Fingerstyle Guitar Tunes

BEAUTIFUL AMERICAN AIRS & BALLADS

Raymond Gonzalez

To access the online audio go to:
WWW.MELBAY.COM/30914MEB

The EM-C guitar model featured on the cover is courtesy of Ed Claxton Guitars.
Photo credit: r.r.jones

WWW.MELBAY.COM

Index

Preface

This collection of 22 lyrical American tunes includes traditional 19th century songs, melodies from the WWII era, plus modern-day pieces by William Bay, president of Mel Bay Publications. The repertoire gave me the opportunity to explore some of the most well-known American ballads as well as to discover songs that I had never heard before.

As always, the arrangements are driven by the melody so they should be easily recognizable. For this collection I used the traditional harmonies as a starting point and didn't venture too far from the main road. Within my arrangements, however, you will likely find unexpected elements which will hopefully add color and surprise to the familiar melodies among them.

All of the settings are in standard or dropped-D tuning and suitable for both steel and nylon-string guitar performance. The unique technical and melodic properties of both types of instruments have been kept in mind to make the arrangements accessible to the intermediate guitarist.

In order to keep page clutter to a minimum I did not indicate fingering or fretboard locations in the standard notation. In addition, where harmonics are featured, I intentionally left out the fret indications. In both instances, please refer to the tablature for string and fret placement.

Whether these tunes are familiar or new to you, I hope the arrangements bring you joy in practice and performance.

All the best,

Raymond Gonzalez

Aura Lee

6-D 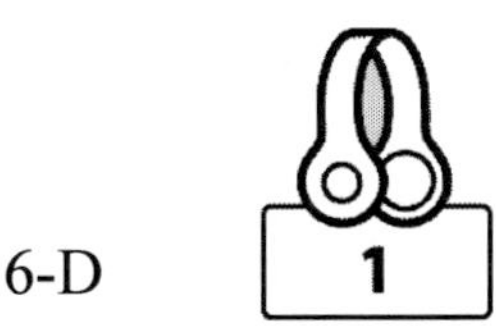

arr. Raymond Gonzalez

A ♩ = 84

Guitar

C
har 12
har 7
II
rall.

Beautiful Dreamer

Freely with rubato

♩ = 104 -110

Stephen Foster
arr. Raymond Gonzalez

A

Guitar

6

11

B *a tempo*

rall.

16

C
a tempo
rall.
D
a tempo
rall.
let bass notes and chords ring

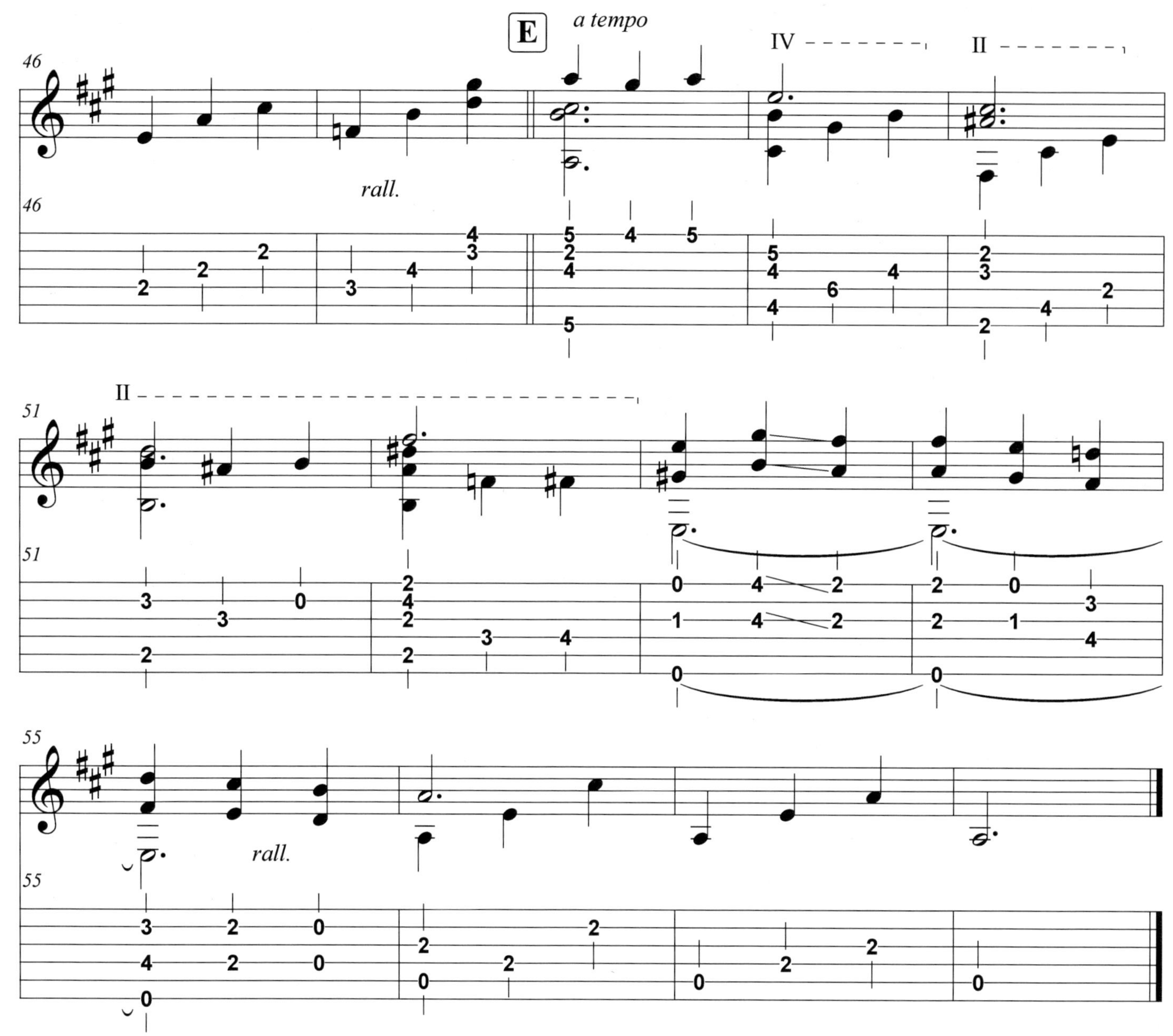
E
a tempo
IV
II
46
rall.
46
51
II
51
55
rall.
55

Black Is the Color of My True Love's Hair

3

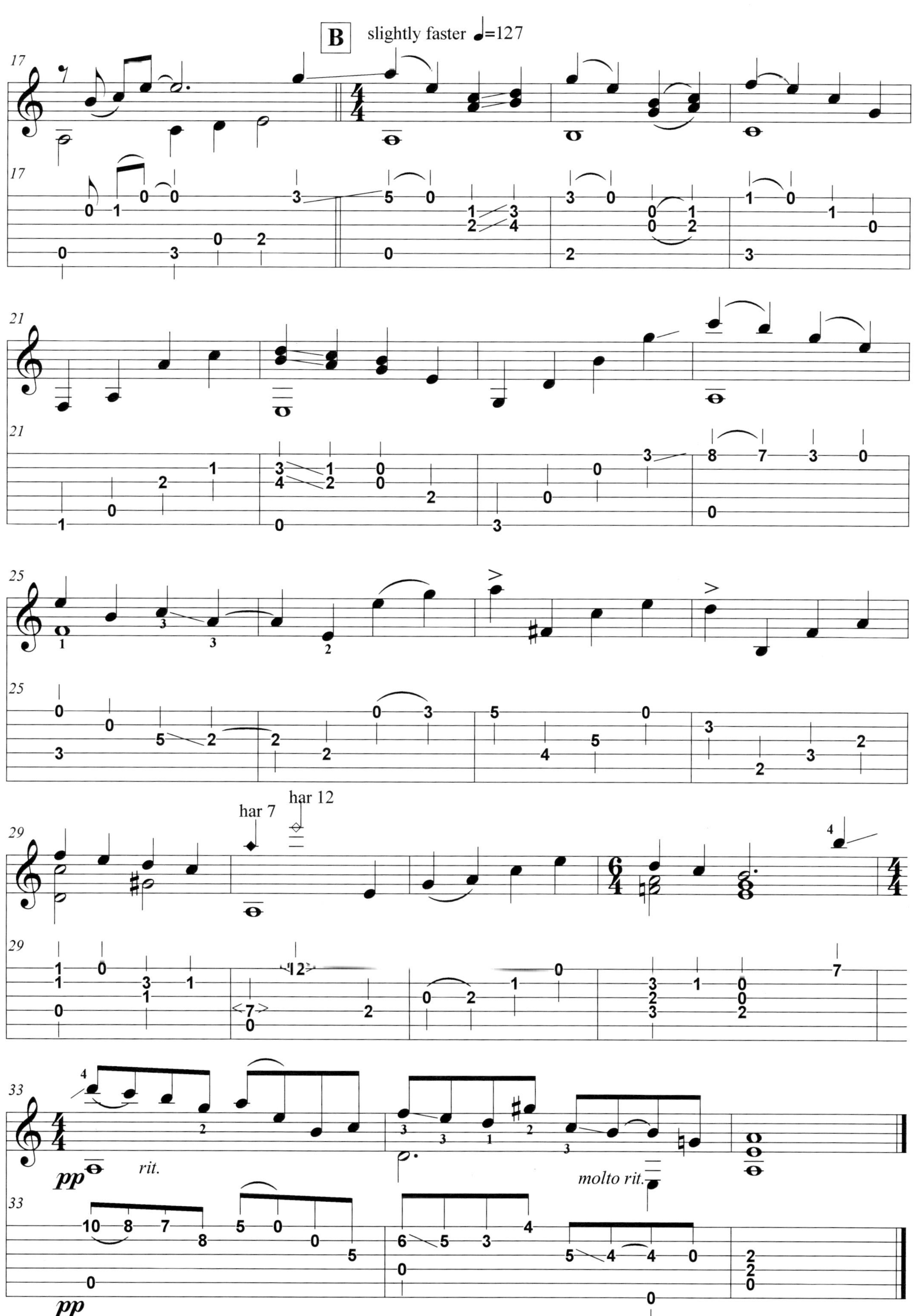
B
slightly faster ♩=127
har 7
har 12
pp
rit.
molto rit.
pp

Black Sunday

Oklahoma, April 14, 1935

William Bay
arr. Raymond Gonzalez

♩ = 84 A

Guitar

T
A
B

4

4

8

B

8

3
4

12

12

C
D
rit.

Darling Nellie Gray

Benjamin Handby
arr. Raymond Gonzalez

Freely

♩ = 70

Guitar

4

8

12

16
1/2VII
IX
VIII
VII
20
24
rall.

Hard Times, Come Again No More

Stephen Foster

arr. Raymond Gonzalez

A ♩=72

Guitar

B

C

a tempo

D

rit.

E
slower
F
rall.

I Dream of Jeanie with the Light Brown Hair

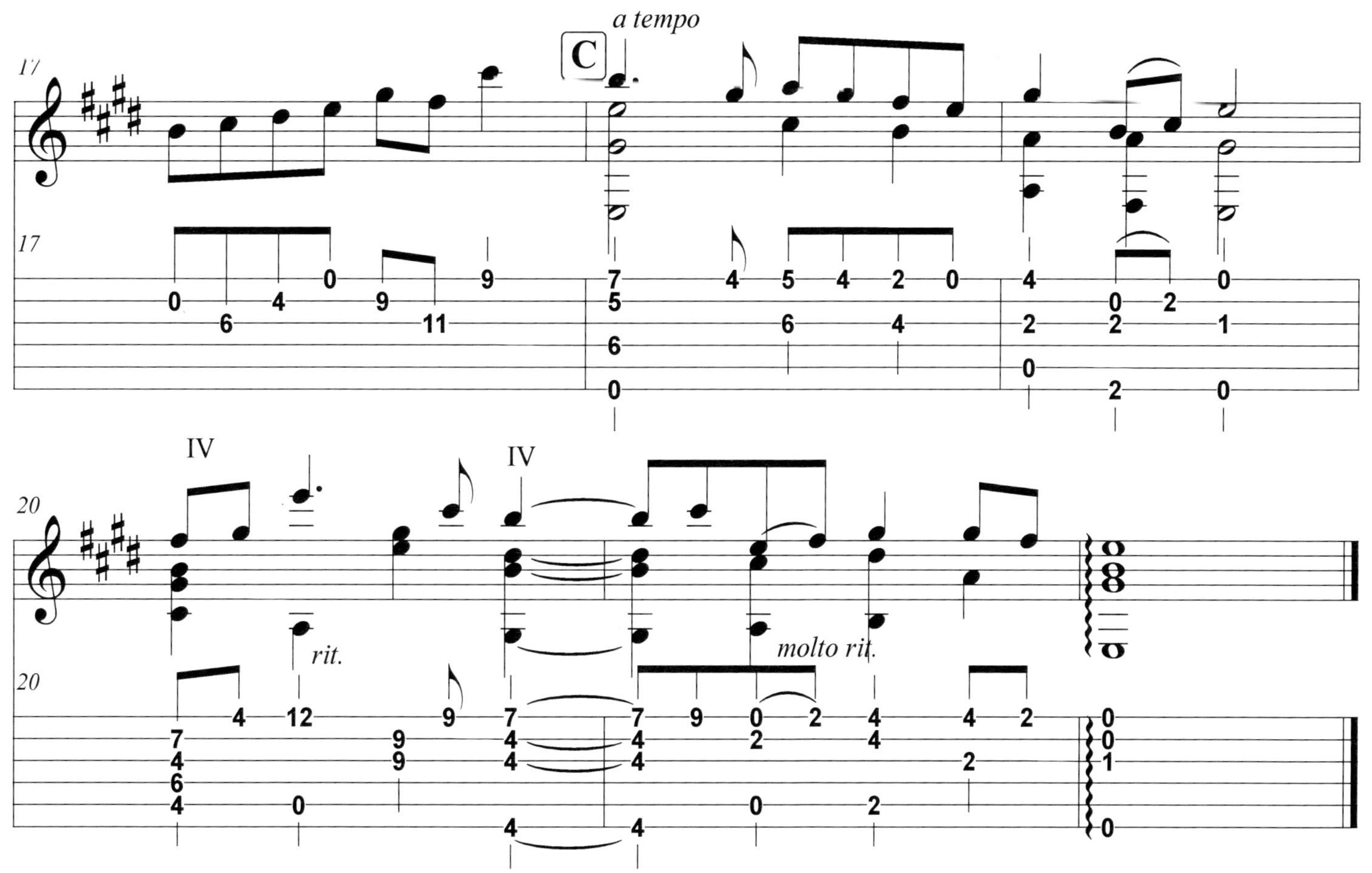
a tempo
C
IV
IV
rit.
molto rit.

In the Pines

arr. Raymond Gonzalez

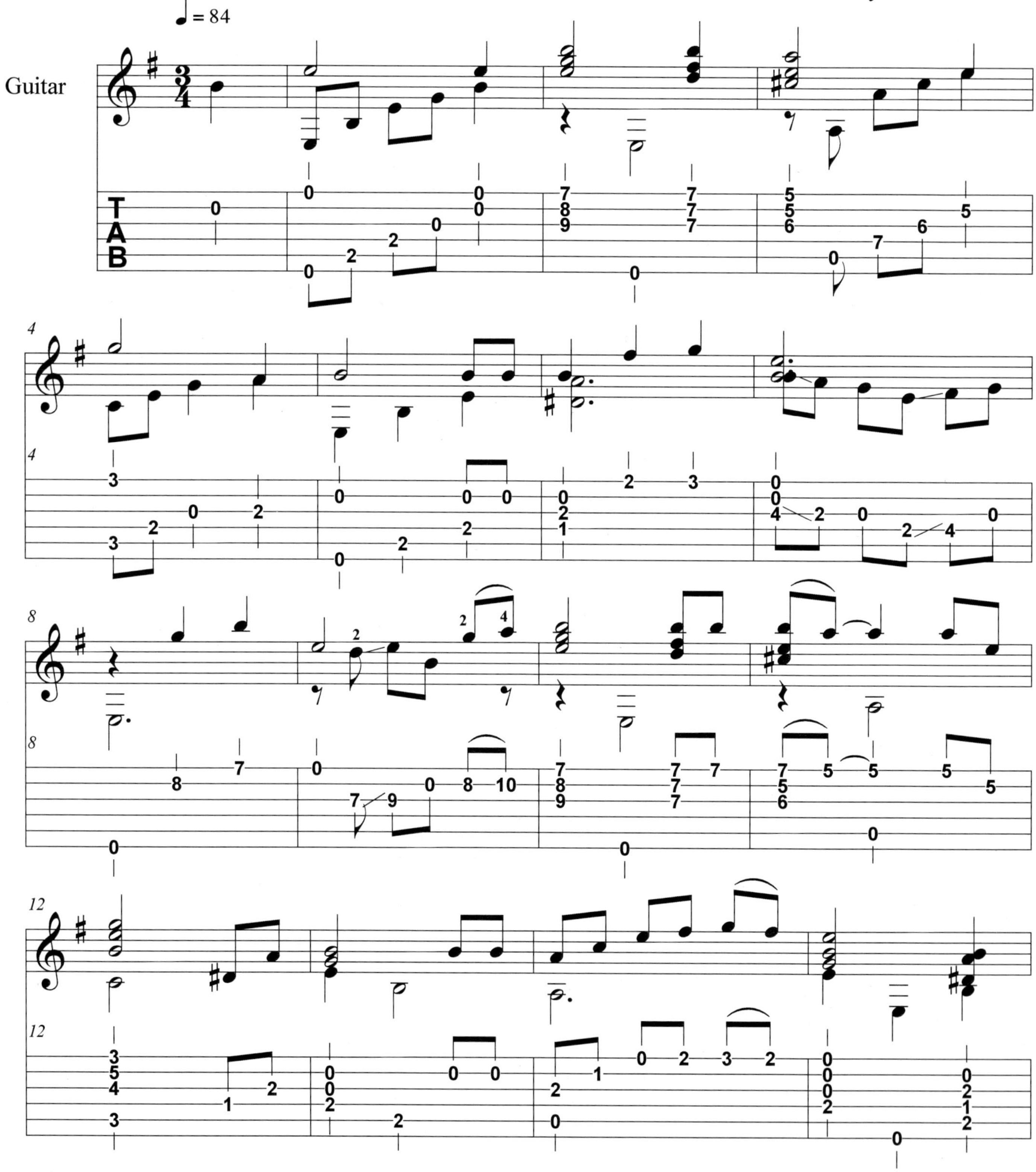

II
har
4/6II
IV
rall.

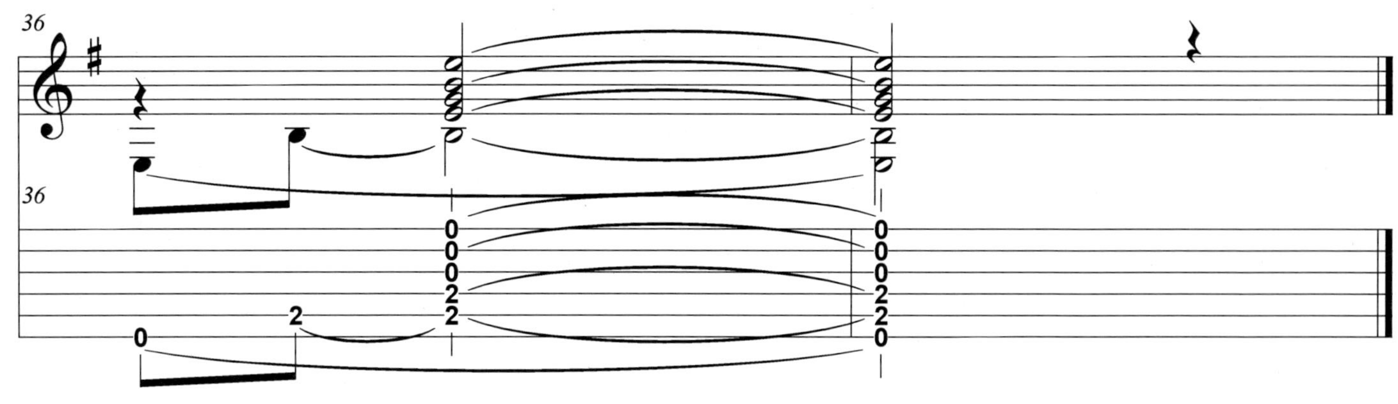
36
36
0
0
0
2
2
0
2
0
0
0
2
2
0

This page has been left blank to avoid an awkward page turn.

Johnny Has Gone for a Soldier

arr. Raymond Gonzalez

H
C
let bass ring
VII
molto rall.

Just Before the Battle, Mother

George F. Root
arr. Raymond Gonzalez

♩=78

Guitar

B

Land of Rest

6-D

arr. Raymond Gonzalez

A ♩= 100

Guitar

4/6 V
VII
II
II
C
let bass notes ring
II
rall.
a tempo

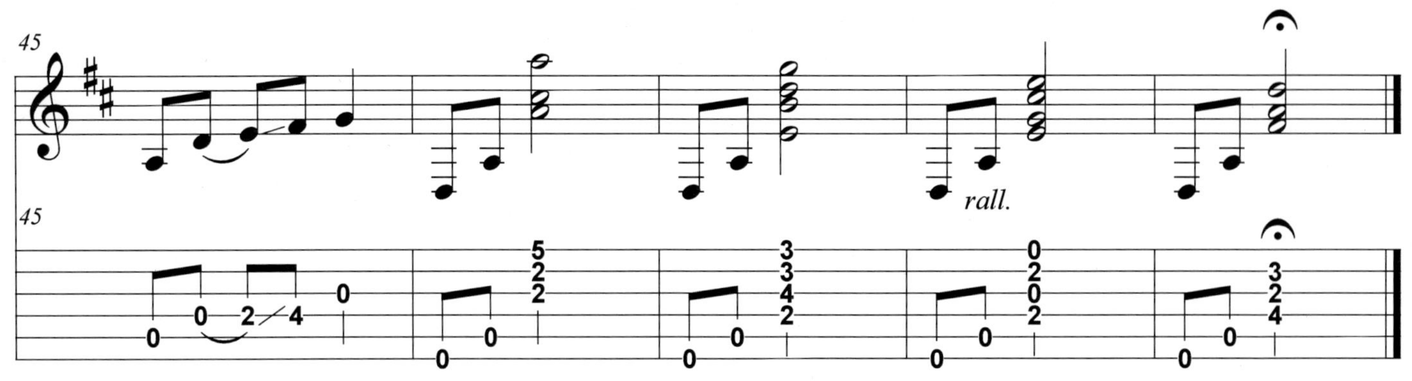
45
rall.
45
0
0
2
4
0
5
2
2
0
0
3
3
4
2
0
0
0
2
0
2
0
0
3
2
4
0
0

This page has been left blank to avoid an awkward page turn.

Lorena

Joseph Philbrick Webster
Rev. Henry D.L. Webster
arr. Raymond Gonzalez

6-D

♩ = 72 **A**

Guitar

T
A
B

4

B

8

II

12

a tempo

rit.

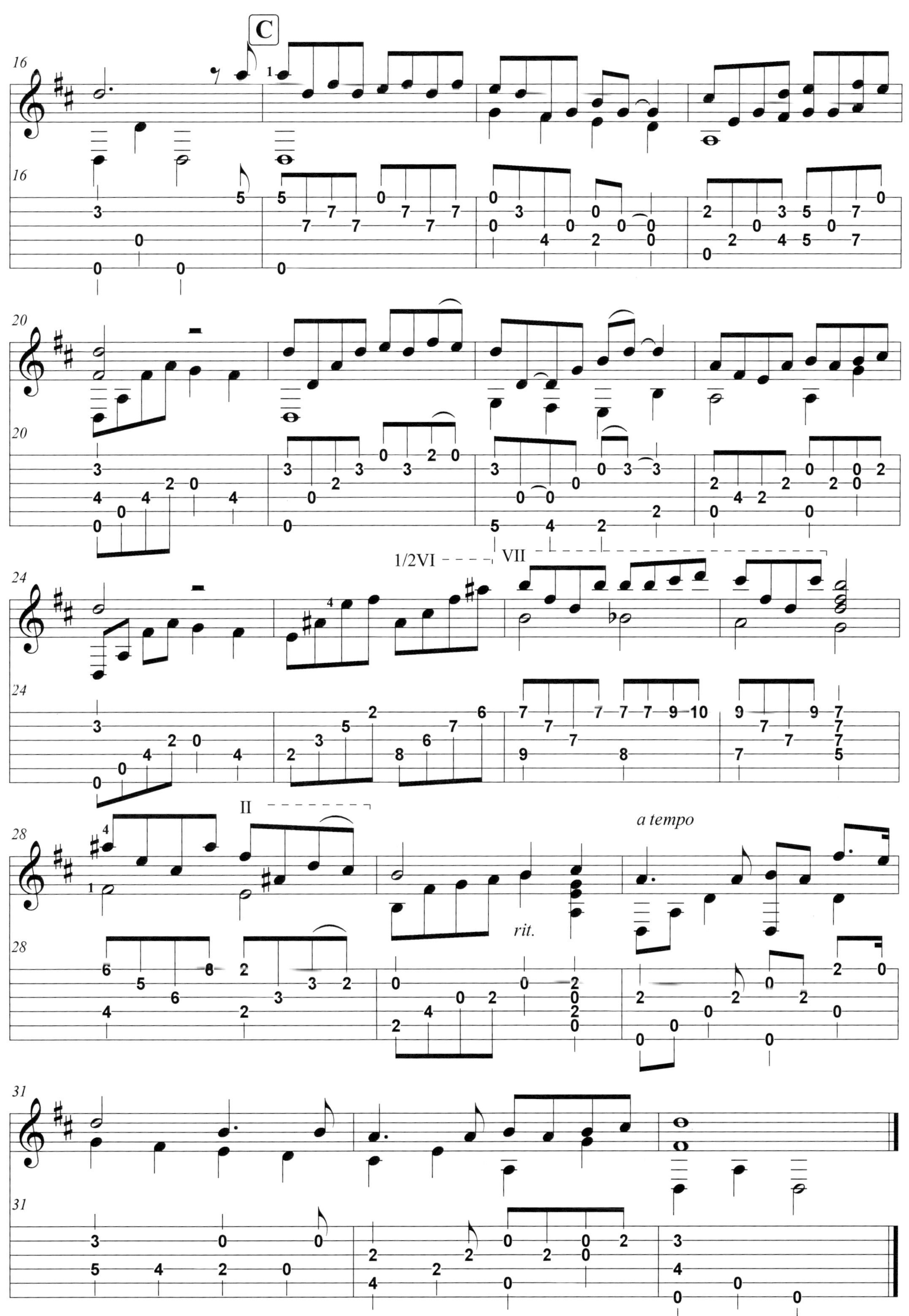
C
1/2VI
VII
II
a tempo
rit.

Paper of Pins

6-D

arr. Raymond Gonzalez

♩=88 A

Guitar

B

II

1/2II

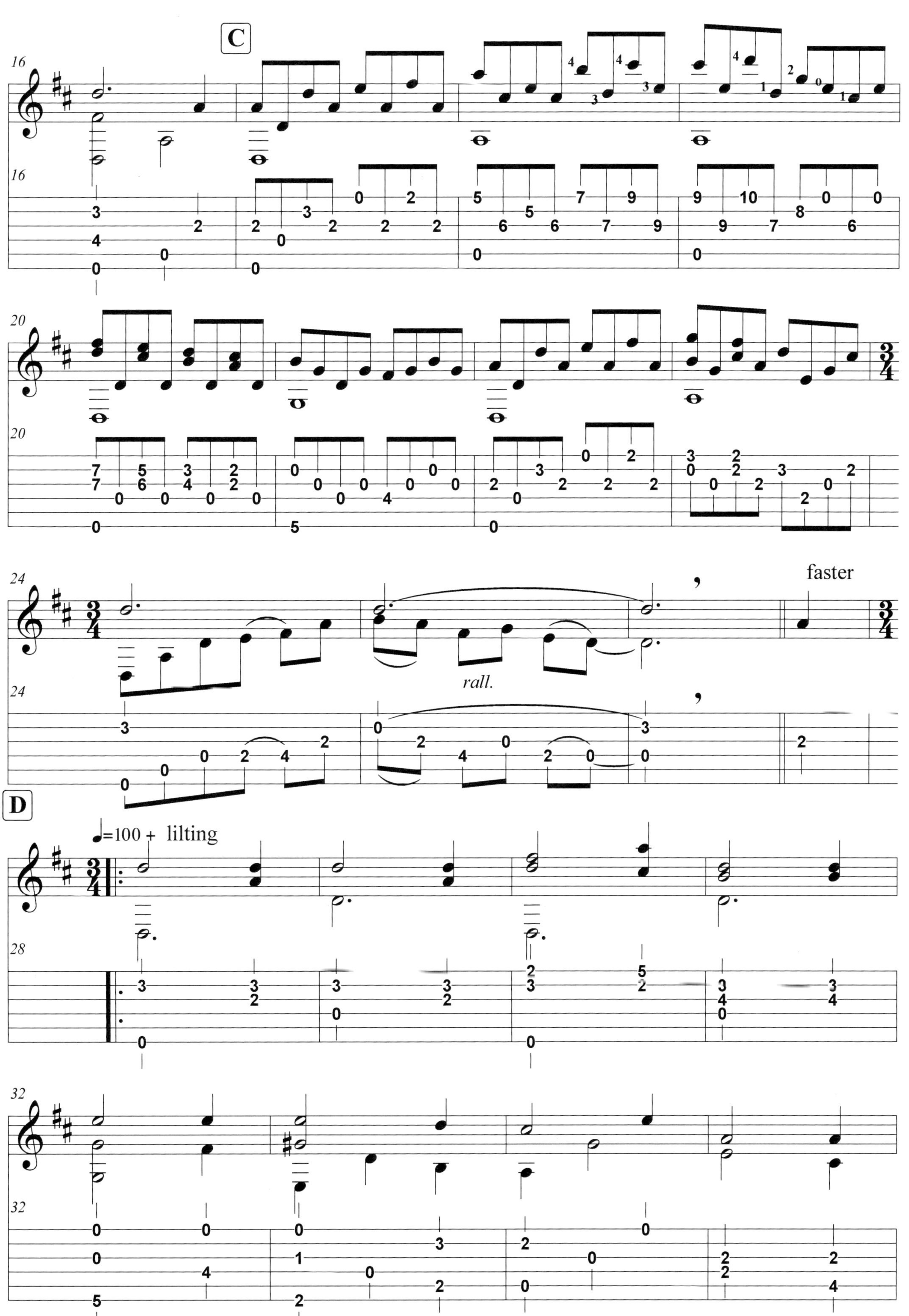
C
D
faster
rall.
♩=100 + lilting

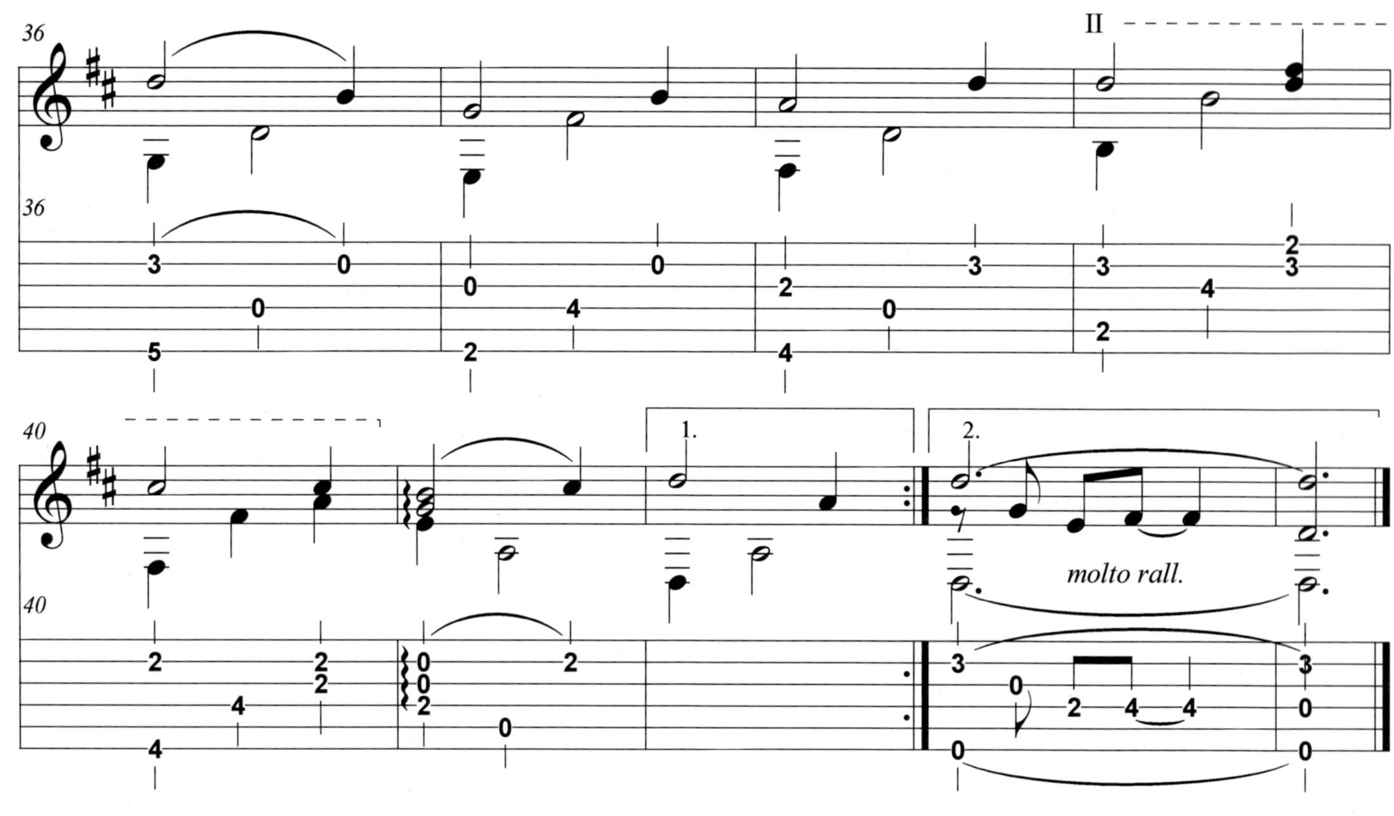
II
1.
2.
molto rall.

This page has been left blank to avoid an awkward page turn.

Prairie Sunset

William Bay
arr. Raymond Gonzalez

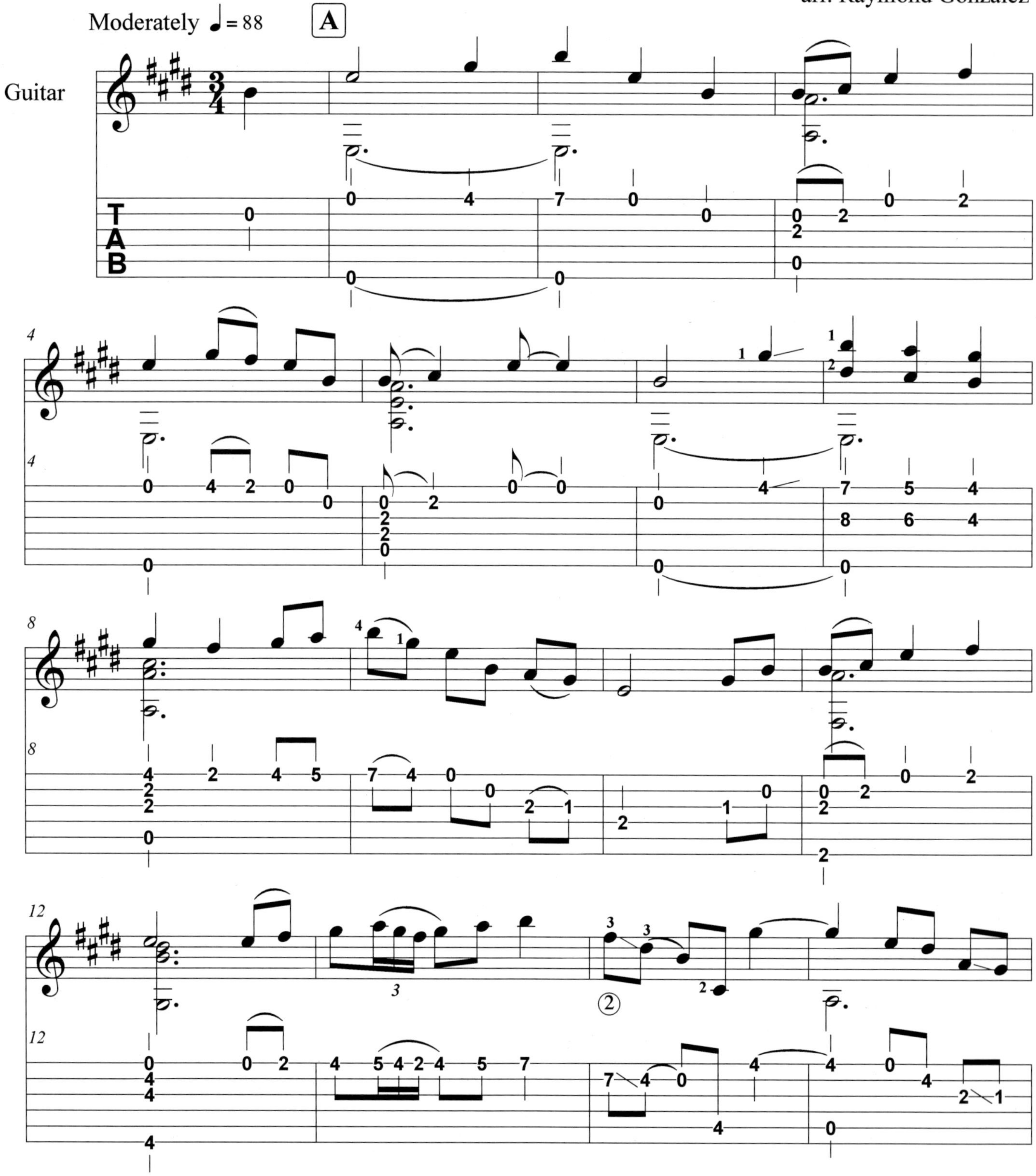

Moderately ♩= 88 **A**

Guitar

B
IV
II

Pretty Peggy - O

6-D

arr. Raymond Gonzalez

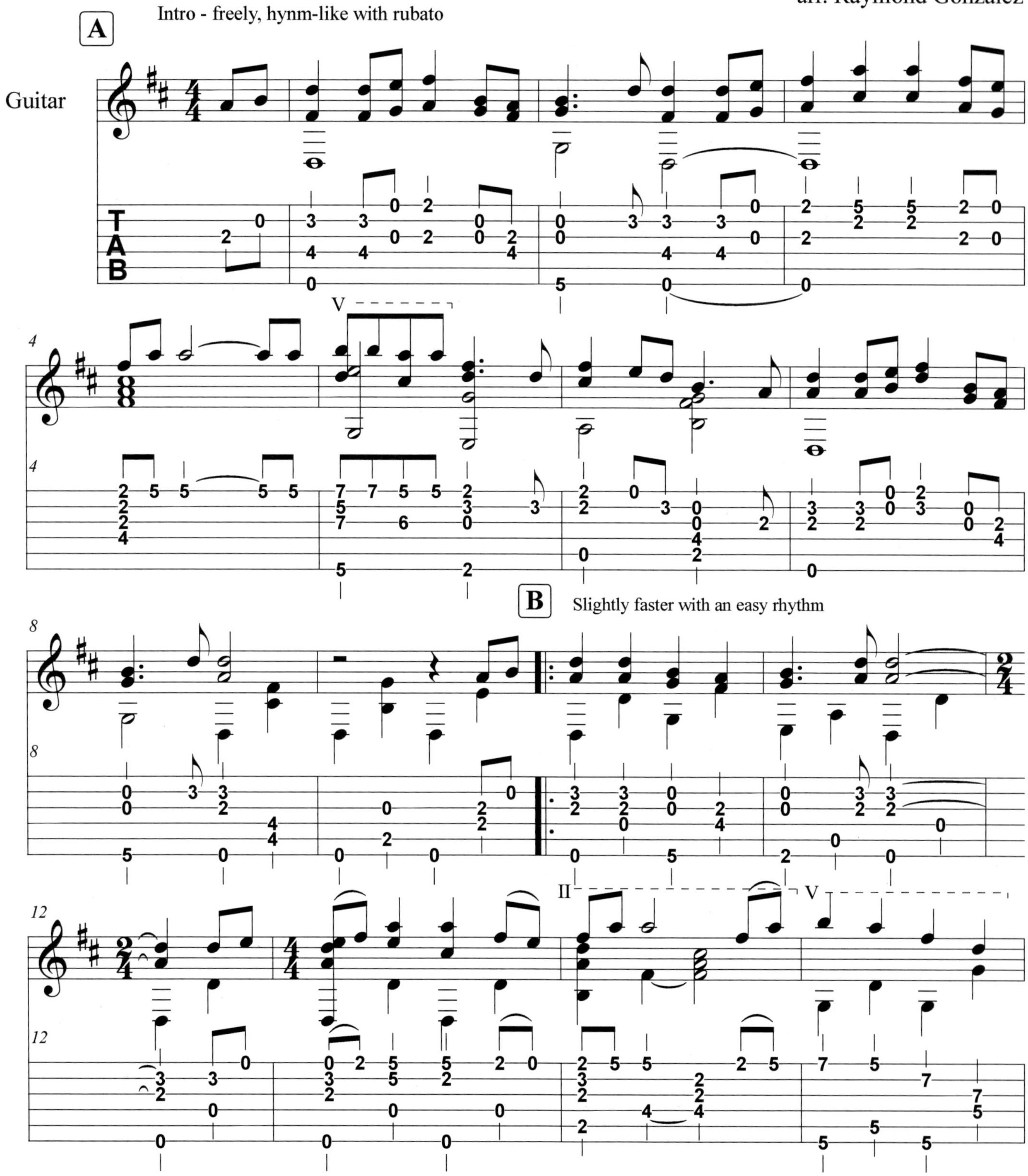

A Intro - freely, hynm-like with rubato

Guitar

B Slightly faster with an easy rhythm

16
1.
16
20
2.
20

Shady Grove

Slow - freely

arr. Raymond Gonzalez

A

Guitar

har 12

Variation 1 - Fast

B

4/6 V

1/2 IX

rit.
C
a tempo
D
Variation 2 - Moderate
rit.

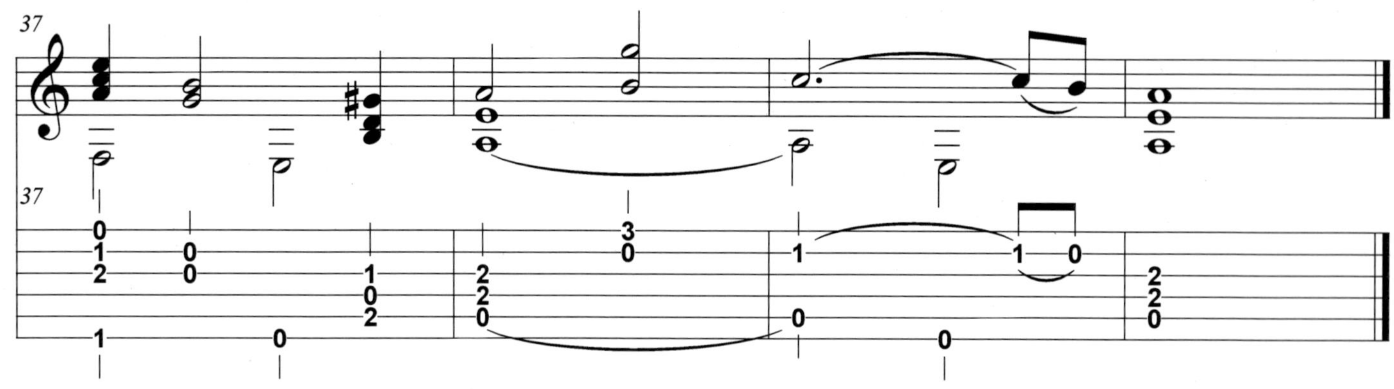
37
37

This page has been left blank to avoid an awkward page turn.

Shenandoah

17

arr. Raymond Gonzalez

16
16
har 7
20
rit.
20

The Lonesome Dove

Appalachian Ballad
arr. Raymond Gonzalez

6-D

♩ = 67-70

A

Guitar

III

4

III I

8

B

12

III

I

1/2V

C

I
III
rall.
hold bass notes

The Long Road

William Bay
arr. Raymond Gonzalez

A ♩ = 70

Guitar

B

C
1/2V
II
har
II
D
rit.

20

The Old Country

William Bay

arr. Raymond Gonzalez

har 12
C

rall.

The Old Homestead

William Bay
arr. Raymond Gonzalez

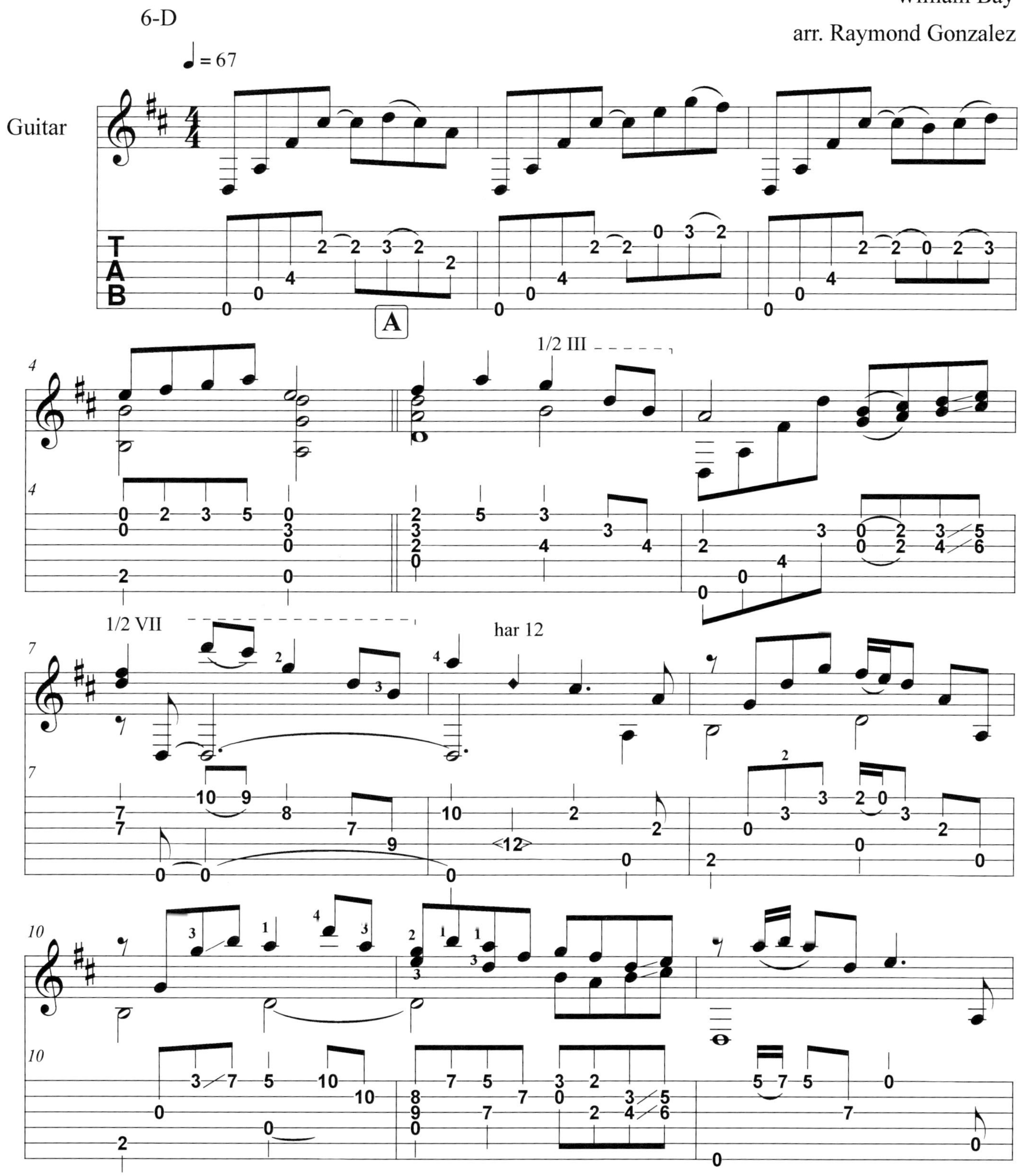

6-D

♩ = 67

Guitar

A

1/2 III

1/2 VII

har 12

har 12
B
rall.
a tempo

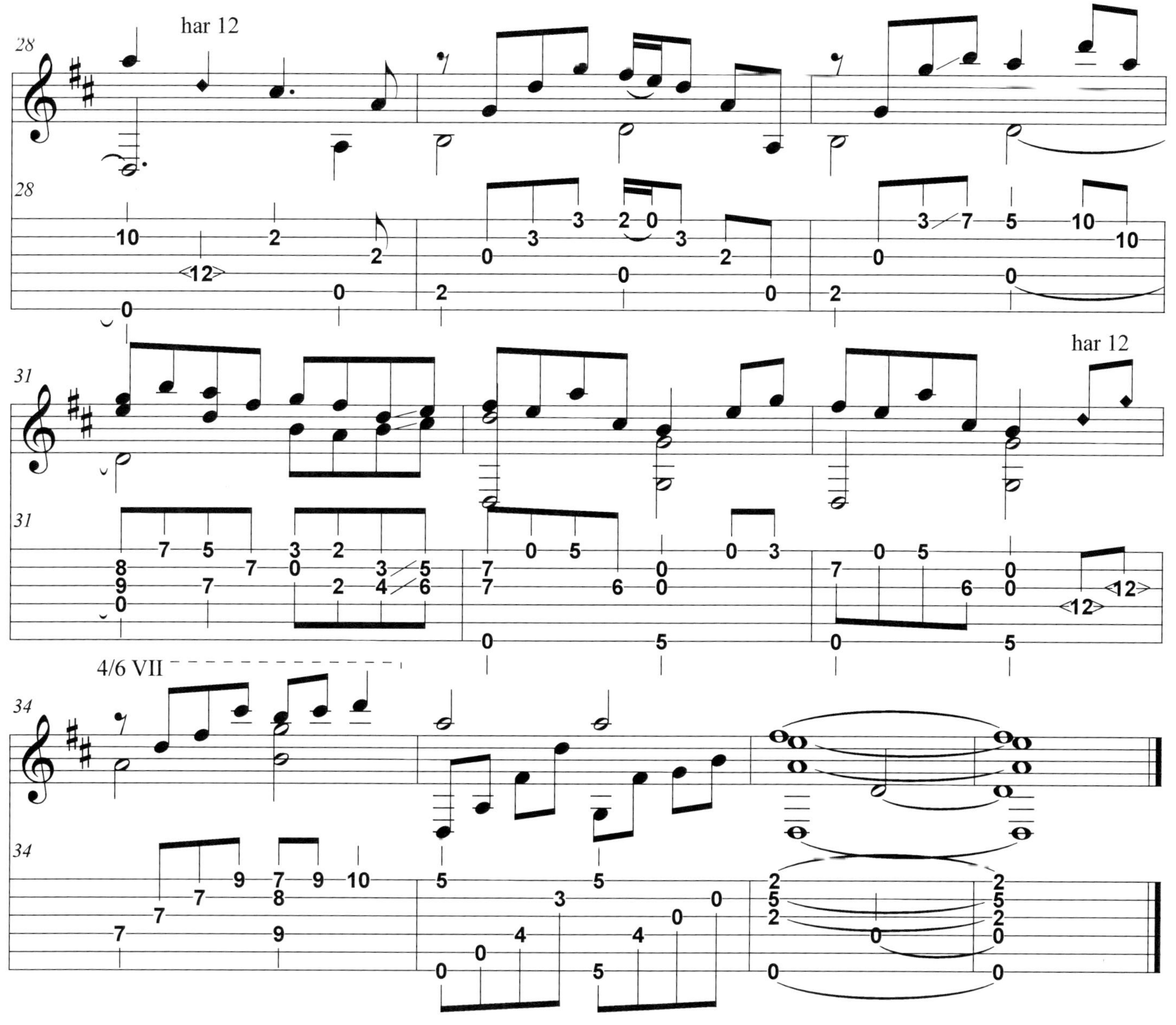
har 12
har 12
4/6 VII

Trail of Tears

William Bay
arr. Raymond Gonzalez

C
1/2 V
1/2 V
D
I
rall.

Other Mel Bay Fingerstyle Guitar Books